Design: Jill Coote
Recipes: Mridula Baljekar
Recipe Photography: Peter Barry
Recipe styling: Bridgeen Deery and Wendy Devenish
Jacket and Illustration Artwork: Jane Winton,
courtesy of Bernard Thornton Artists, London
Editorial: Laura Potts

CLB 3357
Published by Grange Books,
an imprint of Grange Books Limited,
The Grange, Grange Yard, London.
© 1993 CLB Publishing,
Godalming, Surrey, England.
All rights reserved.
Printed and bound in Singapore
This edition reprinted in 1994
ISBN 1-85627-324-5

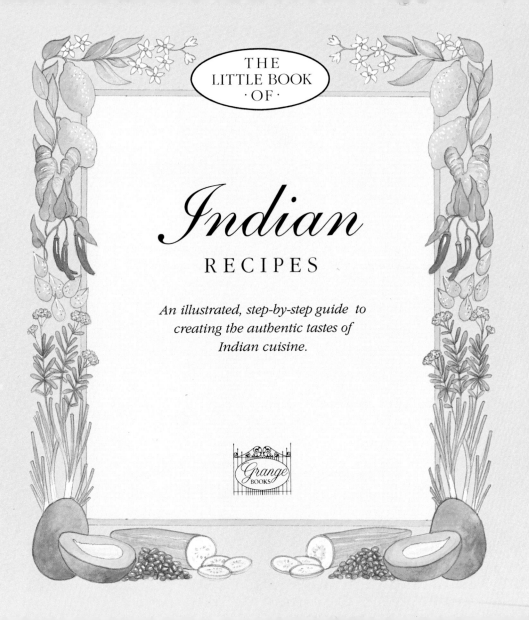

THE LITTLE BOOK ·OF·

Indian

RECIPES

*An illustrated, step-by-step guide to
creating the authentic tastes of
Indian cuisine.*

Grange
BOOKS

Introduction

India is a huge country and its regions were, until recently, very isolated, with poor systems of transport hampering communication. This isolation is reflected in the regional nature of Indian cuisine. Each region made use of the foods that grew locally, particularly spices, and dishes from certain areas developed their own particular characteristics and flavours.

Other factors, aside from regionalism, have influenced the development of Indian cuisine. Over the centuries India has been invaded by many nations, each of which has made a contribution to the style of cookery. The Persian influence, brought to India by the invading Mughals, is particularly marked in northern India, where the dishes are characterised by their delicate flavours and smooth sauces. These textures and tastes are achieved by the addition of coconut and milk or cream, and the use of dried fruit and nuts. The Kashmiris, too, made a notable contribution with their use of saffron and other rare spices. Persian, Greek, Roman, Mongol, Portuguese and British are among the many other cultures that have both given to and learned from the cookery of India.

It is almost impossible to separate the development of Indian cuisine from the religious influences that have shaped the nation. Muslims, for instance, are prohibited from eating pork, and the

consumption of beef is strictly forbidden by Hindus, as the cow is thought of as a sacred animal. Indeed, high caste Hindus in many parts of India are bound by their religion to be vegetarian.

Yet, despite such obvious differences, similar attitudes to food are prevalent throughout India. A selection of dishes is usually served at an Indian meal and these are accompanied by a variety of breads and rice. Traditionally, six *rasas* or flavours – sweet, salty, bitter, astringent, sour and pungent – should be included in every meal. Each of these flavours is believed to have a health benefit of its own, and should be included in a meal in a specific ratio to the other flavours. Indian cooks have long recognised that spices have a value beyond merely flavouring food, and have used these properties to full effect. Spices have a place in Indian cookery both as appetite stimulators and as digestives. Great care, however, is taken to ensure that the spices used in cooking complement, rather than overpower each other.

The recipes in this book cover some of the principal styles of Indian cooking, and give an introduction to the techniques needed to create them. The carefully selected recipes reflect the Indian love of food and give you ideas of how to create and serve authentic Indian dishes.

Chicken Tikka

SERVES 4

The recipe for this popular favourite has been adapted for the conventional oven.

PREPARATION: 30-35 mins, plus time to marinate
COOKING: 15-18 minutes

450g/1lb boneless, skinned chicken breast
1 tsp salt
Juice of ½ a lemon
½ tsp tandoori colour or a few drops of red
    food colouring mixed with 1 tbsp tomato
    purée
2 cloves garlic, peeled and coarsely chopped
½-inch root ginger, peeled and chopped
2 tsps ground coriander
½ tsp ground allspice or garam masala
¼ of a whole nutmeg, finely grated
½ tsp ground turmeric
125g/5oz thick set natural yogurt
4 tbsps corn or vegetable oil
½ tsp chilli powder

---

1. Cut the chicken into 1-inch cubes. Sprinkle with ½ tsp salt and the lemon juice – mix well, cover and keep aside for 30 minutes.

2. Put the remaining ingredients into a liquidiser and blend until smooth.

3. Sieve this marinade over the chicken pieces with the back of a metal spoon until only a very coarse mixture is left.

4. Coat the chicken thoroughly with the sieved marinade. Cover and leave to marinate for 6-8

Step 7 Thread the chicken onto skewers, leaving ¼ inch gap between each piece.

hours or overnight in the refrigerator.

5. Preheat the oven to 230°C/450°F/Gas Mark 8.

6. Line a roasting tin with aluminium foil.

7. Thread the chicken onto skewers, leaving ¼-inch gap between each piece.

8. Place the skewers in the prepared roasting tin and brush with some of the remaining marinade.

9. Cook in the oven for 6-8 minutes.

10. Take the tin out of the oven, turn the skewers over and brush the pieces of chicken with the remaining marinade.

11. Return the tin to the oven and cook for a further 6-8 minutes.

12. Shake off any excess liquid from the chicken.

13. Place the skewers on a serving dish.

Vegetable Samosas

MAKES 18

Vegetable Samosas are a popular Indian snack.

PREPARATION: 60 mins
COOKING: 60 mins

450g/1lb potatoes
2 tbsps cooking oil
½ tsp black mustard seeds
1 tsp cumin seeds
2 dried red chillies, coarsely chopped
1 medium-sized onion, finely chopped
1-2 fresh green chillies, chopped and seeded
½ tsp ground turmeric
1 tsp ground coriander
1 tsp ground cumin
1 tsp salt or to taste
1 tbsp chopped coriander leaves

Pastry
225g/8oz plain flour
50g/2oz ghee or butter
½ tsp salt
75ml/2½fl oz warm water
Oil for frying

1. Boil the potatoes in their jacket, allow to cool thoroughly, then peel and dice them.

2. Heat the oil and add mustard seeds. As soon as they start crackling, add the cumin seeds and red chillies, and then the onions and green chillies. Fry till the onions are soft. Add the turmeric, coriander and cumin.

3. Add the potatoes and the salt. Reduce heat to

Step 9 Fill the cones, leaving about ¼-inch border on the top.

low, stir and cook until thoroughly mixed.

4. Remove from heat and add coriander leaves.

5. Add the butter and salt to the flour. Rub in well.

6. Mix a soft dough by adding the water. Knead until the dough feels soft. Divide the dough into 9 balls. Rotate each ball between your palms in a circular motion, then press it down to make a flat cake.

7. Roll out each flat cake into 4-inch discs and cut into two. Use each semicircle of pastry as one envelope.

8. Moisten the straight edge with a little warm water. Fold the semicircle of pastry in half to form a triangular cone. Join the straight edges by pressing them hard into each other.

9. Fill these cones with the filling, leaving about ¼-inch border on the top. Moisten the top edges and press them together.

10. Deep fry the samosas until golden brown.

Spiced Potato Bites

SERVES 6-8

Delicious sautéed potatoes flavoured with a light sprinkling of spices.

PREPARATION: 30 mins
COOKING: 10-12 mins

700g/1½lbs potatoes
4 tbsps cooking oil
½ tbsp salt
¼ tsp garam masala
½ tsp ground cumin
½ tsp ground coriander
¼-½ tsp chilli powder

---

1. Boil the potatoes in their jacket, cool thoroughly, peel and dice them into 1-inch cubes.

Step 1 Peel and dice the cooked potatoes.

Step 3 Brown the potatoes evenly, stirring them occasionally.

2. In a wide, shallow pan, preferably non-stick or cast iron, heat the oil over medium heat. It is important to have the right pan otherwise the potatoes will stick.

3. Add the potatoes and spread them evenly around the pan. Brown the potatoes evenly, stirring them occasionally.

4. When the potatoes are brown, sprinkle over the salt, garam masala, cumin, coriander and the chilli powder. Stir gently and mix until the potatoes are fully coated with the spices. Remove from the heat.

Fish Bhoona

SERVES 4

For a successful bhoona the spices must be fried until they are a rich brown colour.

PREPARATION: 15-20 mins
COOKING: 30-35 mins

700g/1½lbs steak or fillets of any white fish
6 tbsps cooking oil

Mix the following 4 ingredients in a small bowl
1 tbsp plain flour
¼ tsp ground turmeric
¼ tsp chilli powder
¼ tsp salt

1 large onion, coarsely chopped
½-inch root ginger, peeled and chopped
2-4 cloves garlic, peeled and coarsely chopped
½ tsp ground turmeric
¼ tsp chilli powder
1 tsp ground coriander
½ tsp garam masala
1 small tin of tomatoes
150ml/5fl oz warm water
100g/4oz frozen garden peas
1 tsp salt
1 tbsp chopped coriander leaves

---

1. Skin the fish, wash and dry thoroughly and cut into 2.5 × 5cm/1 × 2-inch pieces.

2. Heat 2 tbsps of the oil in a large frying pan, preferably non-stick, over medium heat.

3. Lightly dust the fish in the seasoned flour and place in the hot oil. Adjust heat to medium-

Step 1 Cut the fish into 2.5 × 5cm/1 × 2-inch pieces.

high. Fry the fish until all the pieces are evenly browned. Drain on absorbent paper.

4. .Put the onion, ginger and garlic into a liquidiser and blend until smooth.

5. Heat the remaining oil over medium heat, add the onion mixture and stir. Heat through, then turn heat down. Fry for 3-4 minutes.

6. Add the turmeric, chilli, coriander and garam masala and fry for 4-5 minutes, stirring continuously. During this time add 1 tbsp juice from the tomatoes at a time to prevent the spices from sticking to the pan.

7. Now add one tomato at a time, along with any remaining juice. Cook until the tomato is well incorporated into the rest of the ingredients.

8. Add the water, peas and salt. Bring to the boil and add the fish. Cover and simmer for 5 minutes, then remove from heat. Garnish with coriander leaves.

Fish Shahjahani

SERVES 4

Fried Brown Rice makes the ideal accompaniment for this rich fish dish.

PREPARATION: 15 mins
COOKING: 15-20 mins

700g/1½lbs fillet of any white fish
75g/3oz roasted cashews
125ml/4fl oz single cream
50g/2oz unsalted butter
225g/8oz onions, finely sliced
2-inch piece of cinnamon stick, broken up
4 green cardamoms, split open the top of each
    pod
2 whole cloves
1-2 fresh green chillies, sliced lengthwise
1 tsp ground turmeric
175ml/6fl oz warm water
1 tsp salt
1 tbsp lemon juice

---

1. Rinse the fish gently in cold water, dry on absorbent paper and cut into 2.5 × 5cm/1 × 2-inch pieces.

2. Put the cashews and the cream in an electric blender and blend to a reasonably fine mixture.

3. In a wide, shallow pan melt the butter over medium heat and fry onions, cinnamon, cardamom, cloves and green chillies until the onions are lightly browned. Stir in the turmeric.

4. Add the water and salt and arrange the fish

Step 3 Fry onions, cinnamon, cardamom cloves and green chillies until the onions are lightly browned.

in a single layer. Bring to the boil, cover the pan and simmer for 2-3 minutes.

5. Now add the cashew/cream mixture and stir gently until the pieces of fish are well coated. Cover the pan again and simmer for a further 2-3 minutes.

6. Remove from heat and gently stir in the lemon juice. Remove cinnamon pieces before serving.

Step 5 Add the cashew/cream mixture and stir gently until the pieces of fish are well covered.

Kheema-Palak
(Mince with Spinach)

SERVES 4-6

Mince and Spinach is a popular Indian dish.

PREPARATION: 15-20 mins
COOKING: 40 mins

4 tbsps cooking oil
½ tsp black mustard seeds
1 tsp cumin seeds
1 fresh green chilli, finely chopped and seeded
  if a milder flavour is preferred
1-inch root ginger, peeled and finely grated
6 cloves garlic, peeled and crushed
450g/1lb lean mince, lamb or beef
1 large onion, finely sliced
2 cinnamon sticks, 2-inches long each, broken up
½ tsp ground turmeric
1 tbsp ground cumin
½ tsp ground black pepper
325g/12oz fresh spinach, chopped or 225g/8oz
  frozen spinach, defrosted and drained
225g/8oz tin tomatoes, drained and chopped
1 tsp garam masala

1. Heat half the oil in a wide shallow pan over medium heat and fry the mustard seeds until they crackle. Add the cumin seeds and immediately follow with the green chilli, ginger and half the garlic. Stir and fry for 30 seconds.

2. Add the mince, stir and fry until all the liquid

Step 3 Add the onions and cinnamon sticks and fry until the onions are lightly browned.

evaporates - this will take 8-10 minutes. Remove the pan from the heat and keep aside.

3. In a separate pan, heat the remaining oil over medium heat and stir in the rest of the garlic. Add the onions and cinnamon sticks and fry until the onions are lightly browned.

4. Adjust heat to low and add the turmeric, cumin and black pepper. Stir and fry for 1 minute. Add the spinach and mix thoroughly.

5. Add the mince and stir until the spinach and the mince are thoroughly mixed. Cover the pan and simmer for 15 minutes.

6. Adjust heat to medium, add 1 tsp salt and the tomatoes, stir and cook for 2-3 minutes.

7. Add the garam masala, stir and cook for a further 2-3 minutes. Remove the pan from heat.

Coriander Chicken

SERVES 4-6

Coriander Chicken is the perfect choice for any dinner party menu.

PREPARATION: 20 mins, plus time to marinate
COOKING: 45-50 mins

1kg/2¼lbs chicken joints, skinned
2-4 cloves garlic, peeled and crushed
125g/5oz thick set natural yogurt
5 tbsps cooking oil
1 large onion, finely sliced
2 tbsps ground coriander
½ tsp ground black pepper
1 tsp ground mixed spice
½ tsp ground turmeric
½ tsp cayenne pepper or chilli powder
125ml/4fl oz warm water
1 tsp salt
25g/1oz ground almonds
2 hard-boiled eggs, sliced
¼ tsp paprika

1. Cut each chicken joint into two, mix thoroughly with the crushed garlic and the

Step 1 Cut each chicken joint into two, mix thoroughly with the crushed garlic and the yogurt.

Step 4 Adjust heat to medium-high and fry the chicken for 5-6 minutes until it changes colour.

yogurt. Cover the container and leave to marinate in a cool place for 2-4 hours or overnight in the refrigerator.

2. Heat the oil over medium heat and fry the onions until they are golden brown. Remove with a slotted spoon and keep aside.

3. In the same oil, fry the coriander, ground pepper, ground mixed spice and turmeric for 15 seconds and add the chicken along with all the marinade in the container.

4. Adjust heat to medium-high and fry the chicken for 5-6 minutes until it changes colour.

5. Add the cayenne or chilli powder, water, salt, and the fried onion slices. Bring to the boil, cover the pan and simmer for 30 minutes until the chicken is tender.

6. Stir in the ground almonds and remove from heat. Garnish with the slices of egg and paprika.

Shahi Korma

SERVES 4-6

This dish is rich and creamy and is a perfect choice for a special occasion.

PREPARATION: 20-25 mins
COOKING: 1 hr 30 mins

1kg/2¼lbs boned leg of lamb, trimmed and cut
   into 1½-inch cubes
125g/5oz thick set natural yogurt
½-inch root ginger, peeled and grated
3-4 cloves of garlic, peeled and crushed
50g/2oz ghee or unsalted butter
2 medium-sized onions, finely chopped

Grind the following ingredients
2 tbsps coriander seeds
8 green cardamoms with the skin on
10 whole black peppercorns
3-4 dried red chillies
1 tsp ground cinnamon
1 tsp ground mace

3-4 tbsps chopped fresh mint
50g/2oz ground almonds
300ml/10fl oz warm water
½ tsp saffron strands, crushed
50g/2oz raw split cashews
150ml/5fl oz single cream
1 tbsp rosewater

1. Put the meat, yogurt, ginger and garlic into a
bowl. Mix thoroughly, cover and leave to
marinate for 2-4 hours.
2. Put the marinated meat, along with any

Step 1 Put the meat into a bowl and add the yogurt, ginger and garlic.

marinade in a heavy-based saucepan. Bring to
a slow simmer, cover and cook for 45-50
minutes stirring occasionally. Transfer the meat
to another container and keep hot.

3. Melt the ghee and fry the onions.

4. Lower heat and add the ground ingredients
and the mint; stir and fry for 2-3 minutes. Add
half of the liquid in which the meat was
cooked, stir and cook for 1-2 minutes. Add the
ground almonds and the remaining meat stock,
stir and cook for 1-2 minutes.

5. Adjust heat to medium and add the meat,
stir and fry the meat for 5-6 minutes.

6. Add water, saffron, 1½ tsp salt and cashews,
bring to a slow boil, cover and simmer for 20
minutes.

7. Add the cream, stir and mix well, simmer
uncovered for 6-8 minutes. Stir in the rosewater
and remove from the heat.

Meat Madras

SERVES 4-6

This hot curry is named after Madras, the major city in southern India.

PREPARATION: 25-30 mins
COOKING: 1 hr 20 mins

---

6 tbsps cooking oil
2 medium onions, coarsely chopped
1-inch root ginger, peeled and coarsely
    chopped
3-4 cloves garlic, peeled and coarsely chopped
4-6 dried red chillies
2 large cloves garlic, peeled and crushed
1-2 fresh green chillies, sliced lengthwise
225g/8oz tin tomatoes
3 tsps ground cumin
1 tsp ground coriander
½-1 tsp chilli powder
1 tsp ground turmeric
1kg/2¼lbs leg or shoulder of lamb, fat removed
    and cut into 1½-inch cubes
175ml/6fl oz warm water
1¼ tsps salt
1 tsp garam masala

---

1. Heat 3 tbsps oil over medium heat and fry the onions, ginger, garlic and red chillies until the onions are soft, stirring frequently. Remove from heat and allow to cool.

2. Meanwhile, heat the remaining oil over medium heat and fry the crushed garlic and green chillies until the garlic is lightly browned.

Step 7 Blend the onion mixture and add to the meat.

3. Add half the tomatoes, along with the juice; stir and cook for 1-2 minutes.

4. Add the cumin, coriander, chilli powder and turmeric, adjust heat to low and cook for 6-8 minutes, stirring frequently.

5. Add the meat and adjust heat to medium-high. Stir and fry for 5-6 minutes until meat changes colour.

6. Add the water, bring to the boil, cover and simmer for 30 minutes.

7. Place the fried onion mixture in an electric blender and add the remaining tomatoes. Blend until smooth and add this to the meat - bring to the boil, add salt and mix well. Cover the pan and simmer for a further 35-40 minutes or until the meat is tender.

8. Stir in the garam masala and remove from heat.

Chapatties

MAKES 14

A chapatti is a dry roasted unleavened bread best eaten as soon as it is cooked.

PREPARATION: 20-25 mins
COOKING: 35-40 mins

325g/12oz fine wholemeal flour
½ tsp salt
1 tbsp butter, or ghee
170ml-280ml/6-10fl oz warm water
1 tbsp extra flour in a shallow bowl or plate

---

1. Food Mixer Method: Place the flour, salt and fat together in the bowl and mix thoroughly at the medium-to-low speed taking care to see that all the fat has been broken up and well incorporated into the flour. Turn speed down to minimum and gradually add the water. When the dough is formed, knead it until it is soft and pliable. Cover the dough with a well-moistened cloth and keep aside for ½-1 hour.

2. Hand Method: Put the flour and salt in a large bowl and rub in the fat. Gradually add the water and keep mixing and kneading until a soft and pliable dough is formed. Cover the dough as above and keep aside.

3. Divide the dough into 14 walnut-sized portions. Roll each portion in a circular motion between the palms to make a smooth round ball, then flatten the ball to make a round cake.

Step 3 Roll each portion of dough in a circular motion between the palms to make a smooth, round ball.

Dip each cake into the dry flour and roll the chapatti into a disc of about 6-inch diameter.

4. An iron griddle is normally used for cooking chapatties, but if you do not have one, use a heavy-based frying pan as the chapatties need even distribution of heat during cooking. Overheating of the pan will cause the chapatties to stick and burn.

5. Heat the griddle or frying pan over medium heat and place a chapatti on it, cook for 30 seconds and turn the chapatti over. Cook until brown spots appear on both sides, turning it over frequently.

6. To keep the chapatties warm, line a piece of aluminium foil with absorbent paper and place the chapatties on one end, cover with the other end and seal the edges.

Tandoori Roti

MAKES 8

Tandoori Rotis, like chapatties, can be served with any meat, chicken or vegetable curry.

PREPARATION: 10-15 mins
COOKING: 25 mins

125g/5oz natural yogurt
450g/1lb plain flour
1 tsp sugar
1 tsp baking powder
½ tsp salt
1½ sachets fast action yeast
1 level tbsp ghee or unsalted butter
1 medium egg, beaten
150ml/5fl oz warm milk

1. Beat the yogurt until smooth, and set aside.

2. In a large bowl, sift the flour with the sugar, baking powder, salt and yeast. Add ghee and mix thoroughly. Add yogurt and egg and knead well.

Step 3
Gradually add the warm milk, and keep kneading until a smooth springy dough is formed.

3. Gradually add the warm milk and keep kneading until a smooth and springy dough is formed.

4. Place the dough in a large plastic food bag and tie up the uppermost part of the bag so that the dough has enough room for expansion inside.

5. Rinse a large bowl with hot water and put the bag of dough in it. Use a steel, metal or enamel bowl as these will retain heat better. Place the bowl in a warm place for ½-¾ hour when it will be almost double in volume.

6. Preheat oven to 225°C/450°F/Gas Mark 8.

7. Line a baking sheet with greased greaseproof paper or baking parchment.

8. Divide the dough into 8 equal-sized balls. Place a ball between your palms and flatten by pressing it down.

9. Dust the ball lightly in a little flour and roll it out gently to a 4-inch disc. Place in the prepared baking sheet. Make the rest of the rotis the same way.

10. Bake on the top rung of the oven for 10-12 minutes. Turn the rotis over and bake for a further 2 minutes.

Mattar Pilau

SERVES 4-6

An easy to prepare pilau rice which has an attractive look provided by the rich green colour of the garden peas.

PREPARATION: 10 mins plus time needed to soak
   the rice
COOKING: 25-30 mins

275g/10oz basmati rice
75g/3oz ghee or unsalted butter
2 tsps fennel seeds
2-3 dried red chillies
6 whole cloves
2 cinnamon sticks, 2-inches long each, broken up
6 green cardamoms, split open the top of each
   pod
2 bay leaves, crumpled
1 large onion, finely sliced
150g/6oz frozen garden peas
1 tsp ground turmeric
1¼ tsps salt
570ml/1 pint water

Step 4 Add the rice, peas, turmeric and salt. Stir and fry until the rice is fairly dry.

·**1.** Wash the rice and soak it in cold water for half an hour. Drain thoroughly.

2. Melt the butter over medium heat and fry the fennel seeds until they are brown.

3. Add the chillies, cloves, cinnamon, cardamom and bay leaves. Stir once and add the onions. Fry until the onions are lightly browned, stirring frequently.

4. Add the rice, peas, turmeric and salt. Stir and fry for 4-5 minutes until the rice is fairly dry, lowering heat towards the last 1-2 minutes.

5. Add the water and bring to the boil. Cover the pan and simmer for 12-15 minutes without lifting the lid. Remove the pan from heat and leave it undisturbed for a further 10-15 minutes. Remove the cinnamon, cardamom pods and bay leaves before serving.

Step 2 Melt the butter over medium heat and fry the fennel seeds until they are brown.

Fried Brown Rice

SERVES 4-6

This traditional rice dish complements Fish Shahjahani perfectly.

PREPARATION: time needed to soak the rice
COOKING: 20-25 mins

275g/10oz basmati or other long grain rice
4 tbsps cooking oil
4 tsps sugar
1 tsp cumin seeds
2 cinnamon sticks, 2-inch long each, broken up
6 whole cloves
6 black peppercorns
2 bay leaves, crumpled
570ml/1 pint water
1 tsp salt

1. Wash the rice and soak in cold water for 30 minutes. Drain well.

2. In a heavy-based saucepan, heat the oil over medium heat and add the sugar.

3. The sugar will gradually begin to change colour to a dark brown. As soon as it does, add the cumin seeds, cinnamon, cloves, black peppercorns and bay leaves. Fry for 30 seconds.

4. Add the rice and fry for about 5 minutes, stirring frequently and lowering heat towards the last minute or two.

5. Add the water and salt. Bring to the boil,

Step 1 Wash the rice and soak in cold water for 30 minutes.

cover and simmer without lifting the lid: 12-15 minutes for basmati rice, 15-18 minutes for other long grain rice.

6. Remove the pan from heat and keep it undisturbed for a further 10-15 minutes before serving. Remove the cinnamon and bay leaves before serving.

Step 3 As the sugar changes colour to dark brown add the cumin seeds, cinnamon, cloves, black peppercorns and bay leaves.

Tarka Dhal
(Spiced Lentils)

SERVES 4

*Dhal is a good source of protein and dhal of some sort is always cooked
as part of a meal in an Indian household.*

PREPARATION: 10 mins
COOKING: 50 mins

150g/6oz Masoor dhal (red split lentils)
750ml/1¼ pint water
1 tsp ground turmeric
1 tsp ground cumin
1 tsp salt
25g/1oz ghee or unsalted butter
1 medium-sized onion, finely chopped
2 cloves garlic, peeled and finely chopped
2 dried red chillies, coarsely chopped

---

1. Put the dhal, water, turmeric, cumin and salt
into a saucepan and bring the liquid to the boil.

Step 2 Reduce heat to medium and cook uncovered for 8-10 minutes, stirring frequently.

Step 4 Remove the dhal from the heat, allow to cool slightly and mash through a sieve.

2. Reduce heat to medium and cook
uncovered for 8-10 minutes, stirring frequently.

3. Now cover the pan and simmer for 30
minutes, stirring occasionally.

4. Remove the dhal from the heat, allow to
cool slightly and mash through a sieve.

5. Melt the ghee or butter over medium heat
and fry the onion, garlic and red chillies until
the onions are well browned.

6. Stir in half the fried onion mixture to the
dhal and put the dhal in a serving dish. Arrange
the remaining fried onions on top.

Cauliflower Masala

SERVES 4-6

This dish is flavoured with a few basic ingredients and the finished dish is semi-dry, making it an ideal accompaniment to rice and curry or Indian bread.

PREPARATION: 25 mins
COOKING: 30-35 mins

1 medium-sized cauliflower
2 medium-sized potatoes
4 tbsps cooking oil
1 tsp cumin seeds
1 large onion
½ tsp ground turmeric
1 tsp ground coriander
1 tsp ground cumin
¼-½ tsp chilli powder
2 ripe tomatoes, skinned and chopped
175ml/6fl oz warm water
100g/4oz frozen peas
1-2 fresh green chillies, seeded and slit
   lengthwise into halves
1 tsp salt
½ tsp garam masala
1 tbsp chopped coriander leaves

1. Cut the cauliflower into florets - wash and drain.

2. Peel and cut the potatoes lengthwise into thick strips about ½-inch.

3. Heat the oil over medium heat and add the cumin seeds. As soon as they start popping,

Step 3 As soon as the cumin seeds start popping, add the onions and fry until they are soft.

add the onions and fry until they are soft.

4. Turn heat down to low and add the turmeric, coriander, cumin and chilli powder. Stir and fry for 2-3 minutes and add the chopped tomatoes. Fry for a further 2-3 minutes stirring continuously.

5. Add the potatoes and the water. Bring to the boil, cover the pan and simmer until the potatoes are half-cooked.

6. Add the cauliflower, cover the pan again and simmer for 10 minutes until the potatoes are tender.

7. Stir in the peas, green chillies, salt and garam masala. Cover and cook for 5 minutes.

8. Remove from heat and stir in the coriander leaves.

Aloo Mattar

SERVES 4-6

Aloo Mattar is a semi-moist potato dish which blends easily with meat, chicken or fish curries.

PREPARATION: 10-15 mins
COOKING: 25-30 mins

4 tbsps cooking oil
1 medium-sized onion, finely chopped
2 cinnamon sticks, each 2-inches long, broken up
½-inch root ginger, peeled and finely chopped
½ tsp ground turmeric
2 tsps ground cumin
¼ tsp chilli powder
¼ tsp freshly ground black pepper
450g/1lb potatoes, peeled and cut into 1-inch cubes
1-2 whole fresh green chillies
1 tbsp tomato purée
1 tsp salt
225ml/8fl oz warm water
100g/4oz frozen garden peas
1 tbsp chopped coriander leaves (optional)

1. Heat the oil over medium heat and fry the onion, cinnamon and ginger for 4-5 minutes, stirring frequently.

2. Reduce heat to low and add the turmeric,

Step 3 Add the potatoes and the green chillies, stir and cook until the spices are blended thoroughly.

cumin, chilli powder and black pepper. Stir and fry for one minute.

3. Add the potatoes and the green chillies, stir and cook until the spices are blended thoroughly (2-3 minutes).

4. Stir in the tomato purée and salt.

5. Add the water, bring to the boil, cover the pan and cook over medium to low heat for 10 minutes until the potatoes are half cooked.

6. Add the peas, cover the pan and cook until the potatoes are tender.

7. Remove the pan from the heat, stir in half the coriander leaves (if used) and sprinkle the remainder on top.

Gobi Mattar
(Cabbage with Garden Peas)

SERVES 4-6

This quick and easy side dish is the ideal accompaniment for Meat Madras.

PREPARATION: 15 mins
COOKING: 10-15 mins

325g/12oz green cabbage
3 tbsps cooking oil
¼ tsp black mustard seeds
½ tsp cumin seeds
10-12 fenugreek seeds (optional)
2-4 dried red chillies, whole
1 small onion, finely sliced
½ tsp ground turmeric
100g/4oz frozen garden peas
¾ tsp salt
1 tsp ground coriander
¼-½ tsp chilli powder
2 small ripe tomatoes, skinned and chopped
1 tbsp chopped coriander leaves (optional)

1. Shred or chop the cabbage finely.

Step 1 Shred or chop the cabbage finely.

Step 6 Add the ground coriander, the chilli powder and the chopped tomatoes.

2. Heat the oil over medium heat and fry the mustard seeds until they pop.

3. Add the cumin seeds followed by the fenugreek (if used), red chillies and the onions. Stir and fry until the onions are soft.

4. Stir in the turmeric and add the cabbage. Stir and mix thoroughly.

5. Add the peas and salt, stir and cover the pan. Lower heat to minimum and cook for 5 minutes.

6. Add the ground coriander, the chilli powder and the chopped tomatoes. Stir until it is completely dry.

7. Remove from heat and stir in half the coriander leaves.

8. Put the cabbage into a serving dish and sprinkle the remaining coriander leaves on top.

Tomato and Cucumber Salad

SERVES 4-6

This salad, with its combination of cucumber, tomato and roasted peanuts makes a mouthwatering side dish.

PREPARATION: 10 mins

½ a cucumber
2 tomatoes
1 bunch spring onions, coarsely chopped
1 tbsp lemon juice
1 tbsp olive oil
¼ tsp salt
¼ tsp freshly ground black pepper
1 tbsp chopped coriander leaves
25g/1oz roasted salted peanuts, crushed

Step 4 Combine the lemon juice, olive oil, salt, pepper and coriander leaves and keep aside.

Step 3 Put the cucumber, tomatoes and spring onions into a serving bowl.

1. Peel the cucumber and chop finely.

2. Chop the tomatoes finely.

3. Put cucumber, tomatoes and spring onions into a serving bowl.

4. Combine the lemon juice, olive oil, salt, pepper and coriander leaves and keep aside.

5. Just before serving, stir in the peanuts and the dressing.

Index

Meat Madras, a hot curry from southern India